Domestic Abuse

Help for the Sufferer

Resources for Changing Lives

A Ministry of
THE CHRISTIAN COUNSELING AND
EDUCATIONAL FOUNDATION
Glenside, Pennsylvania

RCL Ministry Booklets

Domestic Abuse

Help for the Sufferer

Darby A. Strickland

P&R PUBLISHING
P.O. BOX 817 • PHILLIPSBURG • NEW JERSEY 08865-0817

Names: Strickland, Darby A., author.
Title: Domestic abuse. Help for the sufferer / Darby A. Strickland.
Description: Phillipsburg, New Jersey : P&R Publishing Company, [2018] | Series: Resources for changing lives | Includes bibliographical references.
Identifiers: LCCN 2018008375 | ISBN 9781629953250 (pbk.) | ISBN 9781629953267 (epub) | ISBN 9781629953274 (mobi)
Subjects: LCSH: Church work with abused women. | Abused women--Religious life. | Spousal abuse. | Victims of family violence--Religious life.
Classification: LCC BV4445.5 .S77 2018 | DDC 261.8/327 --dc23
LC record available at https://lccn.loc.gov/2018008375

As a biblical counselor, I have seen God place many victims of domestic abuse in my care, and I have learned much from them. My heart carries their stories and their pain. Whether you are a sufferer or someone walking alongside one, you need rich biblical truths, an honest assessment, and sincere wisdom to guide you.

What Is Domestic Abuse?

Domination should not characterize a marriage. God intends marriage to be a place of sanctification, in which we learn to serve, love, and care for each other. Marriage is not supposed to be a place for self-interests; it is designed to be sacrificial—a picture of the relationship between Christ and his redeemed people. If your spouse is seeking to gain or maintain power and control over you, they are violating God's design for the sake of their own dominion. God has a word for this: *oppression*.

The word *oppression* captures the manipulative domination of one person by another. An oppressed person is subject to another's harsh control. God first speaks against oppression when Pharaoh enslaves the Israelites in the book of Exodus. Pharaoh is ruthless and cruel in his domination, enslaving the Israelites to maintain his power. Hearing their cries for help and seeing their suffering, God promises to deliver them (see Ex. 3). Perhaps your spouse is oppressive and you need to know that God sees and hears you—that he has not left you alone without rescue.

Or maybe you are wondering if the trouble in your marriage rises to the level of oppression. Being in a close relationship with another person exposes the flaws in our relationships with God and others. We all fail to love our spouses perfectly because of sin. They fail to love us the way that God desires. We all say and do things we should not. So how do you know when your marriage is bad enough to be considered abusive? You wonder, does the label apply only if physical aggression is present?

Terminology often adds uncertainty. The word *abuse* can describe so many different acts that it leaves many asking, "How bad does it have to be before I can all it abuse?" The same confusion exists over the term *domestic violence*. The justice system and mental health field define this term to include a spectrum of violating acts, including—but not limited to—physical violence.[1] Although I sometimes use the words *abuse* and *domestic violence*, the biblical category of *oppression* emphasizes the domination involved and gives us places in Scripture that speak to your situation.

Oppression in marriage takes place when one spouse seeks to control and dominate the other through a pattern of coercive, controlling, and punishing behaviors. The tactics used by the oppressive spouse can vary. The treatment severely impacts the abused spouse's well-being in ways we will see shortly.

Oppressors come from every culture, race, occupation, age group, and income level. Oftentimes, oppressors are popular and well liked in their roles outside the home. They can even be well-respected leaders in their church. If your spouse is well liked and successful, you may doubt your experience with him or her. You may question your own perceptions and wonder whether *you* are the problem.

Domestic abuse is prevalent.[2] That means that both oppressors and victims attend our churches. Yet many churches fail to talk about oppression. And since it not easily disclosed by victims, it hides in our pews. This may leave you feeling isolated and alone. But you are not alone.

If you are being oppressed, know that Scripture has much to say about your experience, your safety, and God's heart for you. This booklet will help you first to identify abuse and then to understand it, what God says about it, and what you should do about it. We will look at what oppression is, why oppressors oppress, and how their treatment affects you. We'll also explore how you can connect to God and others to get help.

Types of Oppression

Oppression can be hard for you to identify, because it doesn't look the same in every relationship. Different abusers use different behaviors in order to dominate, but we can break down oppression into five general types. As you make sense of what is happening in your marriage, keep in mind that usually more than one type of abuse occurs at a time. Some are subtler than others.

Physical

Physical abuse is the intentional or reckless use of physical force in a way that *may* result in bodily injury or physical pain. It can also be actions that lead to harm—such as refusing sleep or medical care. Physical abuse does not need to cause pain or leave a bruise in order to be considered abusive. A spouse who does anything from throwing things at you or shoving you all the way to choking or beating you is being physically abusive. Physical abuse can be directed at you, your children, or household pets.

Emotional

Emotional abuse (also called mental, verbal, or psychological abuse) is a pattern of behavior that promotes a destructive sense of fear, obligation, shame, or guilt. If your spouse neglects, frightens, isolates, belittles, or exploits you, plays mind games or lies frequently, or blames, shames, or threatens you, they are being emotionally abusive. Repeated personal attacks and manipulations usually result in increased fear, volatility, depression, or even a spectrum of anxiety disorders.

Emotional abuse can be more damaging than physical abuse. It occurs more frequently and distorts the sufferer's perception of themselves and of reality. If you are experiencing attacks on your personhood, you may begin to believe that you are worthless, or even deserving of mistreatment.

Spiritual

Spiritual abuse occurs when the oppressor establishes control and domination by using Scripture, doctrine, or a "leadership role" as weapons. Spiritual abuse can be subtle, as it can mask itself as religious practice. If your spouse exhibits control-oriented leadership, lords power over you, *demands* submission, or uses Scripture in daily life or conflict in shaming and punishing ways, these are signs of spiritual abuse. When a spiritual abuser twists Scripture and uses it to attack, the abuse can feel as though it comes from God himself. Even though the Scripture is out of context, distorted, and weaponized, your oppressor is using

God's words, so it can seem as if God is the one doing the shaming.

Sexual

Sexual abuse happens when sex is not an expression of an emotional or spiritual union. Taken out of God's design, sex is easily corrupted. It is corrupted in the worst way when sex is demanded, required, or taken by force. Obvious categories include rape or forced sex acts. Sex within marriage still requires consent. The *unwanted* intrusion of pornography or implements in sex, undesired sexual activities, peeking or spying, and sexting are abusive acts.

Sex abuse can also be coercive. In such instances, the oppressor uses unrelenting pressure or threats to leverage a sexual encounter after you have already expressed your discomfort or refusal. Sex abuse in a marriage can be very difficult to recognize, and most people I talk to need help in order to understand and identify occurrences. Sadly, a large percentage of my counselees in abusive marriages experience sexual abuse.[3]

Economic

Economic abuse, like other forms of abuse, may be subtle or overt but in general includes tactics that limit the partner's access to assets or family finances or that conceal information. Victims typically have little or no impact on how family resources are spent. The oppressor withholds money in order to control freedoms and relationships, often creating isolation and forced dependency.

Are You Being Oppressed?

The following patterns of behavior are not present in God-honoring and God-fearing people. If you say yes to even one of these questions, you are probably in an oppressive relationship.

Does your spouse ever . . .

- make you feel worthless?
- put you down or call you names?
- look at you or act in ways that scare you?
- hit, kick, shove, slap, choke, or otherwise hurt you, your children, or your pets?
- intimidate and threaten to hurt you or someone you love?
- threaten to hurt themselves because of you?
- prevent or discourage you from seeing your friends and family?
- pressure or force you into unwanted sex or sex acts?
- control your access to money?
- take your money, make you ask for money, or refuse to give you money?

- exclude you from giving input for decisions?
- act jealous or possessive, or constantly accuse you of being unfaithful?
- stalk you, including calling you constantly or monitoring your phone, texts, or email?
- impede or discourage you from going to work or school?
- blame you for their violent behavior or tell you that you deserve it?
- try to control how you spend money, where you go, what medicines you take, or what you wear?
- ignore you for prolonged periods of time?
- threaten you with violence or a weapon?
- use the Bible or doctrine to shame you?
- tell you that you are a bad parent?
- threaten to take away or hurt your children?
- act as if the abuse is no big deal or is your fault, or even deny doing it?
- make you feel afraid to disagree with them or express your opinions?

If you have answered yes to any of the questions above but are still unsure, try considering your situation from another perspective. Ask yourself these questions: How would I feel if this were happening to my daughter, son, or sibling? Would I be okay if someone were treating him or her this way? To gain clarity, ask a wise and trusted friend to consider some of these questions with you.

Cutting through Confusion

People who come to me are often unsure what constitutes abuse. I hear things like, "He only hit me once"; "He's only like that when he's drunk"; "It's reasonable for him to want sex"; "My friend told me I'm making a big deal about nothing"; and "She's just jealous." Sometimes you or people you turn to can overlook, excuse, or deny what is happening. This is especially true when the oppression does not have an obvious physical component. Noticing and acknowledging specific abusive behaviors is an important first step. No one should live in fear of their spouse.

Oppressors want to obscure what they are doing, so they work to create confusion in the minds of their victims. Your uncertainty about what is happening to you and who is to blame perpetuates your oppressor's ability to control and keep you. Almost everyone who is oppressed struggles with confusion, no matter how overt the abuse is. Whether you are beaten, threatened with lethal violence, or emotionally targeted, you probably struggle to maintain clarity about your situation. To make it easier for them to dominate you, oppressors need you to be off balance and disoriented, to believe that you are responsible, and to feel sorry for them.

To cut through the confusion, ask yourself four questions.

Do you feel responsible for your abuse?

Oppressors are masters at playing the victim and making you believe it is your fault that they are angry or hurt. Also, many of their verbal attacks vilify you. If you are hearing things like "If you weren't so stupid I wouldn't be angry!"; "Just look at what I have to put up with!"; or "Stop with all the emotional drama!" over time your spouse's words will make you believe that you are responsible for your spouse's reactions. Nothing could be further from the truth. We all sin and make poor choices, but none of this means that we deserve harsh and cruel punishments from our spouses—ever.

Does your spouse coerce you?

Your oppressor may also confuse you by using coercion, pressuring you to give in and comply with their demands. For example, your husband asks you for sex repeatedly. You know based on past experiences that, if you do not comply, he will lecture you for hours on your "wifely duty," depriving you of sleep, and be frighteningly harsh with your children. To keep peace or stability in the relationship, you must give in.

Coercion is confusing because you ultimately "comply."[4] You do so in order to avoid escalating punishment, but it is very difficult to have clarity about what happens when you conform to a demand. In this example, you may feel as violated as if your spouse had forcefully assaulted you. Yet that feeling may seem unreasonable because, after all, you did "agree to it."

Do you feel sorry for your spouse?

An oppressor may also confuse you by making you feel sorry for them. Oppressors are master blame-shifters. They blame alcohol, drugs, a stressful job, ex-wives, their strong feelings for you—even their mothers. You name it; they use it as an excuse from taking responsibility. Oppressors want you to see them as tortured sufferers. If they can appeal to your kind heart, they hope you will overlook their sins. If that does not work, they may use threats of self-harm or suicide in order to gain your sympathy. Oppressors are very convincing. Keep in mind that they are trying to distract you from the ways that they are deliberately domineering. Understand that making you feel sorry for them is a tactic they use to influence your thoughts and actions. Untangling your oppressor's excuses and threats may require an objective person's help.

Does the abuse come and go?

Abuse has a cyclical nature. Most likely, you do not live under constant full-force attack but rather experience episodic incidents when abusive behaviors are more intense. After abusive incidents, there is a period of time called the *honeymoon period* when your abuser works to "make things up to you." This is where things can become really confusing. When your spouse attempts to repair the relationship, they offer excuses, apologize, blame you, or minimize or deny what happened. During this time, they may appear calm or even express remorse. They may shower you with gifts and affection in an attempt to repair the relationship.

These apparently remorseful actions are usually not true acts of lasting repentance grounded in godly sorrow.[5] Instead, they are attempts to reset the power and control dynamic. Your oppressor's focus remains on what they want. Your oppressor works to control your perception of events by trying to convince you either that they are really sorry, that the abuse was your fault, or that things did not happen in the way you remember.

This is not the behavior of someone who feels sorrow for hurting you. True repentance is more than a confession of sin. The truly repentant person demonstrates an understanding of the impact that their sin has had on you and a humble acceptance of the consequences of their actions (see Ps. 51:3–4). Excuses and blame shifting are a signal that they are still justifying their behavior. Someone who truly wants to be rid of oppressive behavior will enact a plan so that abusive incidents do not reoccur. They will not shift blame. They will take on the responsibility to get help. They will go well beyond an apology and will seek to do actions that lead to restoration. If they truly were horrified at hurting you, they would get help in order to stop being oppressive. They would also try to understand why you are upset with them, giving you time—not pressuring you for forgiveness.

Just after an intense fight, it is easier to see that what happened was wrong. But, over time, your spouse works on your interpretation of the event, and things get cloudy. A period of calm follows the honeymoon phase. On these quieter days, your spouse is helpful and even kind. This is disorienting. During these lighter moments, you may feel bad for not loving your spouse. Maybe you wonder if you have been making a big deal out of nothing. In periods of peace, you may have a hard time recalling the darker moments and may not understand why you now feel cold toward your spouse. Over time, you can come to believe that the incident was your fault or that you have somehow exaggerated what happened.

Sometimes it is difficult to recall how your spouse is dominating, demanding, and demeaning. In these situations, journaling can be useful for gaining clarity. Start keeping a record both of incidents and of what happens afterward. This will help you to keep an accurate record of conflicts so that truth is not obscured and twisted, which will make it easier for you to overcome these disorientations.

What God Says about Oppression

Realizing that you are in an abusive relationship can be frightening and overwhelming. After all, *your spouse*, the one who promised to love and cherish you, is wounding you, controlling you, and, in a twisted way, enslaving you. You wonder, "What should I do?" Just asking the question causes anxiety, since most of the options before you will lead to even more pain and suffering. It seems impossible to stay in a marriage that has become a place of terror and domination.

Coming to terms with the fact that your spouse is violating the very covenant that they made to you, before God, is a devastating reality. But I do not want you to lose hope. God has much to say to comfort you. As we will see here, God does not blame you for your suffering, nor does he tolerate oppression. In fact, he desires to rescue you.

The abuse is not your fault.

Abusive behaviors are inexcusable. They are not the result of your words, actions, or inactions. Nothing you could do could make you deserve or be responsible for abusive treatment—nothing ever. Jesus says,

> What comes out of a person is what defiles him. For from within, out of the heart of man, come evil thoughts, sexual immorality, theft, murder, adultery, coveting, wickedness, deceit, sensuality, envy, slander, pride, foolishness. *All these evil things come from within*, and they defile a person. (Mark 7:20–23).

Your oppressor will blame you for their anger and rage. But Jesus says that these abusive actions come from within them. They will say you provoked them. But God says that the opposite is true. Abusive acts flow from your oppressor's heart, choices, and deliberate actions. Oppressors want to make you feel responsible for their sins so that they can use fear and guilt to control you. But God says it is never your fault. *You cannot make or cause someone else to sin.* We all fail and disappoint our spouses at times, but there are plenty of healthy ways that they can express their hurt. There is no justification for abuse—ever!

You do not deserve this.

Your oppressor hurls accusations at you. These relentless attacks can make you feel that you deserve heinous treatment. Thinking about your failures, you may conclude, "I've not been a faithful Christian, so this is God's way of rebuking me"; "When I was younger, I fell into sin, and I'm paying for it now"; or "If I was a better spouse, God would not need to punish me in this way." These thoughts may leave you believing that you deserve the abuse. However, there is nothing you could have done that would justify oppression. Everything about oppression is unjust. No one deserves to be treated unjustly!

When we are suffering, a common cry of our hearts is to try to understand why something bad is happening to us. Sometimes, when the questions persist, we turn inward and search ourselves, asking, "What did I do to deserve this?" We may think that God is punishing us. But this thinking is false, as it fails to account for God's grace. Our merit, past or present, does not determine God's love and care for us. God's love is for the unlovely and the broken. When we belong to Jesus, grace is based solely on what Jesus has done. Jesus' work is complete, and so we are forgiven—completely. In fact, God says, "I will remember their sins and their lawless deeds no more" (Heb. 10:17). If God does not remember your sins and failings, why would he punish you for them? Jesus, himself, took on the punishment for *all* our sins on the cross. He was lovingly and willingly substituted so that our sins are forgiven and we can be reconciled to God. God's desire is not to punish you but to woo you to himself. He longs to lavish you, flaws and all, with his love-filled grace (see Eph. 1:5–8).

God hates violence.

God is not silent on the issue of violence. Passages such as Psalm 11 describe God's hatred of violent people. Being violent to people, who are made in God's image, does violence to God's image (see Gen. 9:6), so God does not hide his disdain for violence. As we will see in a later section, being married does not mean that you need to stay with a violent spouse. It is not a sin to get away from danger. Nothing in Scripture says that you need to remain in a dangerous situation.

Oppression violates God's design for marriage.

God designed marriage to be a place of mutual trust, sacrifice, care, and honesty. It is supposed to be a reflection of how Jesus loves his church—a relationship characterized by sacrifice (see Gen. 2:23–24; Eph. 5:25, 28–30). Oppressive people make it a place of domination. They have an inflated sense of self-worth and feel that they are owed preferential treatment and unwavering allegiance. They use manipulation and unrelenting pressures to get their needs met. When you fail them, they retaliate. Oppressors are willing to wound you in order to preserve their position of power. This is not what God intended for *any* marriage—not even yours.

You may be thinking, "So what? I'm married, so this is what I have to put up with" or "God hates divorce, so this is my reality!" You are not called to submit to or accept rampant destructive behavior. The opposite is true. You are supposed to help your spouse to know, serve, love, and be more like Jesus (see Col. 3:12–16; 1 Thess. 5:14). That means limiting their ability to sin against you, resisting their domination, and exposing their sin (see Eph. 5:11–14). God does not tell you to put up with an unrepentant sinner.

God sees your suffering.

Oppression is isolating. It can feel like no one, not even God, sees or cares about what is happening to you. The psalmist cries out, "You are the God in whom I take refuge; why have you rejected me? Why do I go about mourning because of the oppression of the enemy?" (Ps. 43:2). The teacher in Ecclesiastes puts it this way: "Again I saw all the oppressions that are done under the sun. And behold, the tears of the oppressed, and they had no one to comfort them! On the side of their oppressors there was power, and there was no one to comfort them" (Eccl. 4:1).

It is natural to wonder if God sees or cares

about your suffering. Take comfort in knowing that Jesus not only sees but also understands your suffering, because he too experienced suffering and oppression: "He was despised and rejected by men, a man of sorrows and acquainted with grief. . . . He was oppressed, and he was afflicted" (Isa. 53:3, 7).

God's desire is to rescue you.

When God talks about oppression, he talks about rescuing his people: "I will rescue my flock; they shall no longer be a prey" (Ezek. 34:22). For God, oppression and rescue are linked together. God does not look on oppression without desiring to deliver his people from it. He says, "I have surely seen the affliction of my people . . . and have heard their cry because of their taskmasters. I know their sufferings, and I have come down to deliver them" (Ex. 3:7). Jesus says that he was sent "to proclaim liberty to the captives . . . to set at liberty those who are oppressed" (Luke 4:18). God encourages you to cry out to him for deliverance, as the psalmist did: "Deliver me, O LORD, from evil men; preserve me from violent men" (Ps. 140:1).[6]

Understanding Oppression's Effects on You

Since everyone responds differently to living in a traumatic situation, it is important for you to recognize what oppression is doing to you personally.

Oppressors use controlling tactics to get their world the way they want it. The subtext is "Serve me or suffer the consequences" or "Give me what I want or you'll get punished!" Living with someone who repeatedly subjects you to their unrelenting desires, expectations, and demands takes a toll. It creates a climate of fear in which you have to work very hard to keep your spouse from becoming angry or retaliating passively (e.g., withdrawing or sulking). This is exhausting, especially since an oppressor's demands are excessive. I have heard the following rules: the family room must always be free of pet hair, you can talk to me for only three minutes, tea must be stirred in a certain direction, I am not to be disturbed by the children when my game is on, you cannot drive more than five miles a day, if you want money for *anything* I need to be asked, and you must work hard to keep from gaining any weight.

Take a moment to consider the demands that your spouse imposes on you. How do they retaliate when you fail to meet their expectations?

If you live with someone who is demanding and punishing, you may feel enslaved, alone, crushed, devalued, resentful, or even angry. It is normal to feel this way. It is likely that there are not many, if any, people you can talk to about what you are experiencing. This leaves you isolated. Perhaps you have withdrawn from people because it is too hard to keep up pretenses or because you feel overwhelmed and depressed. Living with a spouse who attacks you places you on constant alert, promoting fear and anxiety.

Many oppressed people who I speak with struggle with physical intimacy and feel guilty about not having warm feelings toward their spouses. Being dominated does not lend itself to romance! When your spouse abuses you, your heart hurts in deep ways. Memories of those events stick with you. It is hard to trust your spouse or to feel affectionate toward them. You have wounds that are not easily forgotten. Nor should these wounds be forgotten; it is not wise go on interacting with an unrepentant sinner as if they are not a threat or a danger to you. Second Peter 3:17 puts it this way: "Take care that you are not carried away with the error of lawless people and lose your own stability."

Sometimes the strain of living with an oppressor affects the body. When we are not free to talk about the things that hurt us or we are unable to make sense of our experience, our bodies sound the alarm for us. I have known women who get migraines in the afternoon before their husbands come home. Their bodies anticipate the coming stress and react even before they are able to make a cognitive correlation.

Take a moment to list any physical symptoms that you experience. Keep a record of them. They are an important indicator of how you are doing. Headaches, stomachaches, and anxiety are the symptoms I encounter most regularly. But symptoms can include sleeping and eating too much or too little, panic attacks, pervasive pain throughout the body, neck and chest pain, trouble swallowing, urinary tract infections, depression, and irritability.

A word of caution: sometimes it is tempting to turn to alcohol, drugs, or an affair to cope with the anxiety, isolation, and emptiness. These ways of coping are harmful and make you more vulnerable to danger. Nor do they honor God. At the same time, it makes sense that you would seek an escape from the nightmare you are living in. Later in this booklet, I will provide you with some strategic things you can do to address your suffering and some wise steps you can take. If you are struggling with destructive ways of coping, enlist help so you can find real and lasting rescue.

Understanding the Heart of an Oppressor

Until you understand why your spouse is oppressive, you will be prone to blame yourself, hold on to false optimism, make excuses for your spouse's sin (and thus endure more harm), or believe that if you change the abuse will stop. But these beliefs leave you vulnerable to more attacks and subject you to increasing domination. It is vital to your safety and sanity to understand how oppressors think.

Oppressors believe that they are entitled to certain things and treatment. Perhaps your spouse demands sex very frequently or desires the house to be impeccably clean. They may require you to spend all your free time with them at the exclusion of other family and friends. Maybe they have strong ideas about how each dollar is spent, or they micromanage you in other ways. One thing is clear: their preferences and desires trump yours. Worse, they believe that it is your job to keep them happy—in every way meeting their desires and demands. Put simply, oppressive people enforce a form of slavery in their homes.

Oppressors are effective manipulators because they portray themselves as sufferers. For example, they might excuse their behavior by saying that they feel slighted by you, criticized, jealous, under pressure at work, or wounded from another relationship. I want to impress upon you that oppression stems from attitudes and values—not feelings.[7] Oppressors do not do abusive things because they feel bad; rather, they oppress because they have an entitled mentality.[8] Their sense of entitlement does not come from feelings of inferiority or past pain. Rather, op-pressors have an inflated sense of themselves that allows them to justify mistreating others so that their demands are met. Oppressors may want you to think that they lose control, but instead they are taking control.

Oppressors have little self-awareness and are profoundly self-deceived about their own behavior and intentions.[9] They see things completely dif-ferently from others, which makes arguing with them nearly impossible. They think they are right and their behavior is justified. They do not see their brokenness, so nothing internal propels them to change. What then would motivate them to give up the "rewards" and control that their abusive behaviors grant them? If things are going to improve with your oppressor, you need to be the one to take action or get help.[10]

The contrast between Jesus and your op-pressor is jarring. Jesus came into the world sac-rificially. He was willing to empty himself, even to the point of death, in order to display his love for you. He does not hold his power and position over you but shows sacrificial devotion for you. He does not dominate you, demand your affections, or subject you to his majesty, but he woos you with his gentle and forgiving love. Look to Jesus as a sweet reminder of what love is and what he wants for you. Because of his love for us, Jesus was willing to be wounded and to give up power. In stark contrast, oppressors wound others in order to preserve their power and secure their entitlements.

Monitoring Your Safety

Sin intensifies over time. Continual and unrepentant sin causes hearts to grow hard. Desensitized hearts not only perpetuate sin, they magnify it. Thus, abuse often becomes more severe and frequent over time. Abuse may escalate so gradually that it is difficult for you to see what is happening until it becomes more severe. Other times it progresses quickly and catches you off guard. It is important for you to consider your safety.

Physical and sexual abuse can and probably will increase over time. What started as blocking or pushing can become kicking, choking, or a beating that leaves you severely wounded. Sometimes physical abuse may be lethal. *Violence does not de-escalate*. If your spouse has hit you, chances are that in the next physical altercation the violence will pick up with the same or greater intensity.

Sex abuse can also be progressive. For example, what starts out with sexual jokes and pressure leads to your spouse treating you as a sex object, then touching you in ways that feel violating. Sex abuse can also become dangerous, even lethal—especially if your spouse forces sex after an argument. Many Christian women who I work with were raped by their spouse or forced into sexual acts. Few things are more terrifying.

It is difficult, if not impossible, to predict if or when an oppressor's use of violence will escalate to the point of homicide. Serious injuries (either intentional or accidental) are more probable as the abuser uses more and more dangerous types of abusive behaviors. Please take time to note the frequency and levels of violence you have experienced, as well as any escalations.

Another word of caution: it is quite possible that a nonviolent abuser will become violent over time. Be alert to this and be prepared. If you find yourself in danger, never hesitate to leave or call 911.

Should You Flee?

Continually evaluate the level of danger you are in, ideally while working with someone who is very familiar with domestic violence.[11] If you are experiencing violence of any kind, you are living in an unsafe situation. The occurrence of violence is unpredictable and should not be tolerated. But I also want you to know that you do not have to be experiencing physical abuse in order to leave. *All the behaviors* described in this booklet are intolerable and inexcusable. Again, I would urge you to enlist help in thinking through your situation.

Leaving is the most dangerous time in an abusive situation, but sometimes it is the wisest course of action. It is ideal if you can consult with people who understand oppression and understand how oppressors operate. A wise person will consider your safety over everything else. Usually I have to help my counselees talk to their pastors or elders so that they understand not just the current situation but also how a spouse might react or retaliate if they are exposed. Make sure those who are helping you know the potential for escalation and retaliation. Many well-meaning people may suggest marriage counseling or want you or someone else to talk with your spouse about the abuse, but it is not always wise or safe to confront an abuser. No matter how small the confrontation might seem, it can add volatility.

Here are some things you need to consider:

- Is the best course of action for you (and your children) to flee a dangerous spouse? If the answer is yes and fleeing is necessary, it is usually safest to leave without giving any indication that you are doing so.
- Can you take time to plan to leave? Or do you have to leave immediately? If

your situation allows, you may be able to gather important papers, consult for legal advice, and make other preparations. Some people I have worked with planned for a few months to leave; others had to leave quickly. Each situation is different.

- If you need to leave, who can you trust to help you and keep the secret? If you are working with a church, make sure they know to keep the circle of people who are aware of the situation very small. Ask them to seek out resources if they need help navigating your need to leave or the steps involved. Good and caring pastors and elders will be open to learning how to help.

- You may realize that your situation is bad, but you may not be ready to leave, not want to leave, have reasons for not leaving, or be afraid to so do. I would urge you to talk to someone, as you will need ongoing support, safety monitoring, and wisdom.

If You Decide to Flee

You may be wondering, "Is it okay to leave? God hates divorce. Won't I be sinning against God if I leave?" It is never wrong or sinful to flee danger.[12] Jesus did so (see Matt. 2:13–14;

John 8:58–59; 11:53–54), and the apostle Paul repeatedly fled abusive and dangerous situations (see Acts 9:22–25; 14:5–7; 17:8–10, 14).[13]

In particular, though, the example of Abigail reminds us that wives are not called to submit to dangerous husbands. When Abigail's husband, Nabal, made an unwise and selfish stand against David, he placed her and her entire household in danger. Abigail wisely disregarded her husband's unrighteous actions and sought protection. God honored her bravery, and Nabal's foolishness led to his demise (see 1 Sam. 25).

Abigail went behind her husband's back and against his authority in order to save her entire household. If you are in a dangerous situation, you too need to seek protection and care. Like Abigail, you need to be furtive and cautious. You should carefully prepare for your escape and create a safety plan.[14] Cover your tracks. Assume that your spouse is monitoring your cell phone, computer, and other electronic trails. Remember, leaving is the most dangerous time for you, so it is best if you have help and logistical support.

You may be thinking, "What if my spouse hasn't caused me physical harm? Sure, it's easy to see that physical violence is wrong, but isn't my spouse's sin something that I am called to endure?"

Scripture says,

There are six things that the LORD hates,
    seven that are an abomination to him:
haughty eyes, a lying tongue,
    and hands that shed innocent blood,
a heart that devises wicked plans,
    feet that make haste to run to evil,
a false witness who breathes out lies,
    and one who sows discord among
    brothers. (Prov. 6:16–19)

Oppressors do these things. Lundy Bancroft writes,

> The scars from mental cruelty can be as deep and long-lasting as wounds from punches or slaps but are often not as obvious. In fact, even among women who have experienced violence from a partner, half or more report that the man's emotional abuse is what is causing them the greatest harm."[15]

God hates what is being done to you. If your oppressor is unwilling to make important and significant changes, God does not require you to endure oppression while waiting for change. You will need much wisdom in order to figure out the best course of action in your particular situation. But recognize that God does not want you to suffer in such intense and dehumanizing ways.

If you have children, talk to someone about the unique ways that this situation causes them to suffer. Many people I have worked with stayed with their oppressors because they thought it was best for their children. However, over time they could see the negative effects that living amidst abuse had on their children. Children can suffer from depression or anxiety, develop behavior problems, experience increased risk for using drugs and alcohol, struggle in school, believe they are responsible, get injured in the cross fire, or have difficulty forming healthy relationships. Many of my counselees watched their children turn away from the Lord, especially when spiritual abuse had taken place or when the oppressive parent proclaimed to be a believer, preforming well in public but being a terror in private. Pray for your children and contemplate these verses: "I have set before you life and death, blessing and curse. Therefore choose life, that you and your offspring may live, loving the LORD your God, obeying his voice and holding fast to him" (Deut. 30:19–20).

Perhaps you have compelling reasons to stay with your oppressor: lack of resources or support, fear of retaliation, hope for change, concerns about your children, belief that you should stay, love for your spouse, or the desire not to disappoint yourself and others. It is important for you to seek out support. I believe that God will make it clear to you over time what is best for you to do given your situation.

Fleeing danger does not necessarily mean divorce. It can mean many things, including separation or temporary escape. Ultimately, whether you choose to stay or to flee, it is critical that you build support systems and self-care strategies.

Speaking to Others

The evils of domestic violence thrive behind closed doors. One reason they persist is that no one sees what is happening to you. Your abuser knows that if others were aware of what they are doing, it would cause them tremendous problems. That is why they typically do not abuse you in public and why they threaten to harm you if you reveal what is happening.

When you are isolated, it is possible that you will believe the lies of your oppressor and remain in a fog of confusion. God says that it is not good to be alone. This is especially true when you are oppressed. He desires you to have help from wise and loving people. God calls you to bring abusive acts into the light so that you may be rescued (see Eph. 5:11, 13). This will not be easy. You may be concerned that no one will believe you because your spouse is deceptively charming. You may have already tried reaching out to friends and church leaders, only for them to minimize your pleas for help or, worse, blame you for the acts of your oppressor.

Domestic violence is terrifying both to experience and to reveal. Here are a few things to consider that may help you find appropriate support.

Sometimes it's necessary to go outside your church in order to seek help. Many loving and supportive churches care well for the oppressed, guiding and protecting them. Yet, sadly, the church has not always been a place of refuge for the oppressed. Sometimes teaching on submission and hyper-headship, mutuality in all marriage problems, "wifely duty" regarding sex, and gender roles produces more wounds and contributes to a church's misunderstanding of the dynamics of oppression. Unfortunately, churches can fail to protect their precious sheep. Be on guard for this. If someone tells you that you are experiencing abuse because you are not submissive or because of your own sin, seek help elsewhere. In other cases, your church community may not be properly educated, have a bad track record with domestic abuse, or lack the resources to help you. You may worry that your spouse will learn that you are exposing their abuse before you are ready and safe. Seek places and resources that understand oppressive dynamics. You need safe places and people.

Wise and loving people will take the time to listen to your entire story. Like Jesus, they will enter in. They will not tell you not to speak about your spouse without your spouse present or accuse you of slander. They will seek to draw you out, asking for more examples and showing appropriate concern. Wise people will not minimize, dismiss, or excuse the abuse of an oppressor. People who are committed to loving you well, even if they do not understand what is happening to you, will take the time to learn about abuse or will connect you to people or resources that show understanding. Pray that God would reveal to you the person or people who have the capacity to care for you appropriately. Be discerning when you approach people for help; if you feel misunderstood or blamed, reconsider your choice. One way to identify the right person is to ask what they have read about abuse. Share an article, this booklet, or a blog post with them and see what they think about it.

Your spouse's presentation and ability to deceive may be an obstacle for people who know them. It may take friends some time before they grasp what you are telling them about your spouse. Allow for this, but know that a true friend will believe what you are telling them.

Look for people who track with you and are willing to wait with you as you figure out how to manage your situation. It is not helpful to seek advice from people who want to tell you what to do or who shame you for not doing what they would do. Your spouse already does this to you! People who care about you will be afraid for you and may urge you to take actions that you are not ready for. Don't be afraid to speak up. Remind them that you are different from them and that you need more time or want to handle things a different way.

Financial resources and isolation often stand in the way of seeking help. If this is the case, see if you can find a free local support group, or make use of domestic violence hotlines. Sometimes it is wise to tell your spouse that you need counseling in order to deal with one of the side effects of the oppression, such as depression or anxiety. If your depression or anxiety is adversely affecting their world, they may agree to it. Consider asking your church to contribute to counseling or babysitting so that you can make important support connections.

Speaking to God

Oppression may leave you feeling as though God is far from you. One of the psalmist's biggest fears is that God has turned his face from him. Even when you are upset with him and feel abandoned, God invites you to speak to him, even using such words as these: "Why, O LORD, do you stand far away? Why do you hide yourself in times of trouble?" (Ps. 10:1). God wants to know and care for your heart. He has even given you the Holy Spirit, your Comforter, to help you turn to him with your deepest pain.

God does not ask us to forget our suffering. Quite the opposite is true. He invites us to lament. The Psalms are full of cries to the Lord, from his people in anguish. Sometimes it is helpful to find a psalm that captures your heart and to use it to cry out to God. (Psalms 18, 22, 55, 56, and 57 are particularly relevant.) Lamenting is a powerful way of worshiping God, because it helps you to remember God's love for you even in the worst of circumstances.

God understands the deep betrayal that can come from a close companion. He gives you language to both express your anguish and plead for justice:

> For it is not an enemy who taunts me—
> > then I could bear it;
> it is not an adversary who deals inso-
> > lently with me—
> > then I could hide from him.
> But it is you, a man, my equal,
> > my companion, my familiar friend.
>
> . . . .
>
> Let death steal over them;
> > let them go down to Sheol alive;

for evil is in their dwelling place and
in their heart. (Ps. 55:12–13, 15)

Use these words, pleading with the Lord
that your tormentor would know the evil and
pain that they have caused. While this seems
harsh, it is the beginning of repentance. Your
spouse needs to become aware of the damage
they have caused, to understand the ruin they
have made, and to see the death they have
brought to your marriage. God understands the
destruction; he sees it. It is good to speak to
God about the anger, resentment, and hope-
lessness you feel. Plead with him for the justice
you desire and for your spouse to be repentant.
He knows your heart, and he understands the
torment you feel when your own spouse is
wounding you. You do not need to have san-
itized speech in order to plead with the Lord;
bring him your whole heart.

Sometimes the most beautiful prayers are
the simplest and shortest. Crying out "Help
me" shows your dependence and trust. God
promises to be a refuge for the oppressed (see
Ps. 9:9). He says, "Fear not. . . . I am the one
who helps you . . . ; [I am] your Redeemer"
(Isa. 41:14). Trust God to hear the cries of your
heart. Talk to him about what hurts. He will
hear your cry.

Seeking help from God means, in part,
remembering who he is and who you are to

him. Your oppressor would like you to believe that you are not worthy of Jesus' love and redemption. Your spouse's criticism, threats, and mockery are a profound betrayal. You have endured a horrendous kind of tearing down and shaming when the messages you receive from your spouse proclaim your worthlessness. It can be easy to believe the lies when they come from the one closest to you. When you feel unlovable and unworthy, it is hard to remember how God sees you.

The truth is that when God speaks of you, he rejoices over you. He promises you that "you shall be called by a new name. . . . You shall be a crown of beauty in the hand of the LORD. . . . You shall no more be termed Forsaken . . . but you shall be called My Delight Is in Her. . . . So shall your God rejoice over you" (Isa. 62:2–5). Let that sink in for a minute. God says that you are a crown of beauty and that his delight is in you. Bask in the truths of who God says you are. You are precious to him. His voice needs to become louder than the voice of your oppressor.

Tune your heart to listen to him. Look to God to discover who he says you are. If you are one of his people through faith, he calls you a treasured possession (see Deut. 7:6), chosen and holy (see Col. 3:12), beloved (see Deut. 33:3), his child (see 1 John 3:1), a friend (see John 15:15), holy and blameless (see Eph. 1:4), and redeemed (see Eph. 1:7). The depth of his love for you propels him into motion for you—not simply redeeming you from your sins (as if that were not enough) but also rescuing you from your oppressive marriage. Let David's words be an encouragement to you:

> I sought the LORD, and he answered me
>   and delivered me from all my fears.
> Those who look to him are radiant,
>   and their faces shall never be ashamed.
>   (Ps. 34:4–5)

Look to Jesus in the midst of your suffering. Let him tell you how valuable you are to him, and let these truths propel you into action.

Next Steps

Comprehending and processing all of this takes time. I hope that you will continue to reflect and pray about your situation with the knowledge that God cares deeply about you. If possible, seek counsel from a wise person who has experience with helping victims of domestic abuse. Keep in mind that you show love to your spouse and honor God when you bring your spouse's sin into the light (see Eph. 5:11). The abuses that you suffer are too intense to endure without support and help.

Sometimes taking this next step feels

overwhelming. Talking about these things can be hard. Even though you are not responsible for what your oppressor has done to you, it may still feel shameful to talk about them. Perhaps you can bring this booklet with you and share both what you have learned and questions that you still have.

If you are not ready to talk to someone you know, begin by praying about who you may confide in, by journaling, or by calling the anonymous domestic violence hotline (1-800-799-SAFE; you can also chat online at http://www.thehotline.org/help/).

Stay focused on one key truth: in sacrificing his Son for you, God shows that he holds nothing back from you. He delights in redeeming and rescuing—especially his heartbroken children.

Darby A. Strickland (MDiv, Westminster Theological Seminary) *is a counselor who teaches others, at CCEF and at churches, how to counsel abusive marriages and care for the abused.*

Further Resources

Books

Holcomb, Justin S., and Lindsey A. Holcomb. *Is It My Fault? Hope and Healing for Those Suffering Domestic Violence*. Chicago: Moody Publishers, 2014.

Strickland, Darby A. *Domestic Abuse: Recognize, Respond, Rescue*. Phillipsburg, NJ: P&R Publishing, 2018.

Safety Planning Resources

"Get Help." Onelove. Accessed January 6, 2018. https://www.joinonelove.org/get-help/.

"Leaving an Abusive Relationship," Woman's Health, accessed January 6, 2018, http://womenshealth.gov/violence-against-women/get-help-for-violence/safety-planning-for-abusive-situations.html.

National Crisis Organizations and Assistance

National Child Abuse Hotline / Childhelp
1-800-422-4453 (1-800-4-A-CHILD)
www.childhelp.org

**National Dating Abuse Helpline /
Loveisrespect**
1-866-331-9474
www.loveisrespect.org

The National Domestic Violence Hotline
1-800-799-7233 (SAFE)
www.thehotline.org

**National Resource Center on Domestic
Violence**
1-800-537-2238
www.nrcdv.org and www.vawnet.org

National Sexual Assault Hotline
1-800-656-4673 (HOPE)
www.rainn.org

National Suicide Prevention Lifeline
1-800-273-8255 (TALK)
www.suicidepreventionlifeline.org

Legal Help

**American Bar Association Commission on
Domestic & Sexual Violence**
1-202-662-1000
www.americanbar.org/groups/domestic
_violence.html

Battered Women's Justice Project
1-800-903-0111
www.bwjp.org

Notes

1 The US Department of Justice defines domestic violence as a pattern of abusive behavior in any relationship that is used by one partner to gain or maintain power and control over another intimate partner. Domestic violence can be physical, sexual, emotional, economic, or psychological actions or threats of actions that influence another person. For their full definition, see "Domestic Violence," The United States Department of Justice, updated June 16, 2017, https://www.justice.gov/ovw/domestic -violence.

2 Nearly one in three women in the United States (30.3%) has been slapped, pushed, or shoved by an intimate partner at some point in her lifetime. Approximately one in four women in the United States (24.3%) has experienced *severe* physical violence by an intimate partner in her lifetime (see "The National Intimate Partner and Sexual Violence Survey: 2010 Summary Report," National Center for Injury Prevention and Control and Centers for Disease Control and Prevention, November 2011, http://www.cdc.gov/violenceprevention/pdf/nisvs _report2010-a.pdf, pp. 43–44).

3 Sexual assault or forced sex occurs in approximately 40–45 percent of battering relationships (see "How Widespread Is Intimate Partner Violence?" National Institute of Justice, accessed January 10, 2018, https://www.nij.gov/topics/crime/intimate-partner -violence/pages/extent.aspx#noteReferrer5).

4 Coercion is the practice of forcing another person to perform or behave in an involuntary manner (through either action or inaction) by use of threats,

intimidation, or other use of force or pressure. So it is contradictory to believe that complying was truly voluntary. "Coerced consent" is an oxymoron.

5 Godly regret is focused on how sin offends God, and it produces true repentance (see 2 Cor. 7:10).

6 To read about other instances when God shows his care for the oppressed, see Genesis 16; 1 Samuel 25; Psalm 146:7–9; Isaiah 1:17; Jeremiah 50:33–34; Zechariah 7:10; and Luke 4:18–19.

7 See Lundy Bancroft, *Why Does He Do That? Inside the Minds of Angry and Controlling Men* (New York: Berkley Books, 2003), 75.

8 Entitlement is the core attitude of oppressors. For a detailed discussion of entitlement, see my article "Entitlement: When Expectations Go Toxic," *Journal of Biblical Counseling* 29, no. 1 (2015): 19–33.

9 Violent people neither know themselves nor let others know them (see Jer. 17:9).

10 While Christians can draw on the Holy Spirit and have hope for change, it is important to consider that the majority of abusers, even those in the best abuse programs, do not change. One reason for this is the intrinsic rewards that come with being abusive. Change would mean giving up the many benefits that come with dominating another. For more on the process of change and what steps toward change would look like, see Bancroft, *Why Does He Do That?*, 334–61.

11 There are several tools for this. I use the myPlan app from the One Love Foundation. You can also make use of local community resources such as the police or domestic violence shelters; the National Hotline (1-800-799-SAFE) can also refer you to local resources.

The biggest predictors of lethal violence are if you believe your spouse is capable of killing you or if your spouse has previously attacked or threatened you with a weapon, strangled (choked) you, forced sex, threatened to harm or kill themselves, or been violently jealous. If these have happened, make use of the above resources.

12 For an in-depth look at this, see Justin and Lindsey Holcomb's article "Does the Bible Say Women Should Suffer Abuse and Violence?," *Journal of Biblical Counseling* 28, no. 2 (2014): 9–21; or their book *Is It My Fault? Hope and Healing for Those Suffering Domestic Violence* (Chicago: Moody Publishers, 2014).

13 See also Holcomb and Holcomb, *Is It My Fault?*, 127–43.

14 For a safety planning worksheet, see "Domestic Violence Personalized Safety Plan," National Center on Domestic and Sexual Violence, accessed June 15, 2016, http://mnadv.org/_mnadvWeb/wp-content/uploads/2011/07/DV_Safety_Plan.pdf.

15 Bancroft, *Why Does He Do That?*, 8.

RCL Ministry Booklets

Booklets by Jeffrey S. Black, Michael R. Emlet, Walter Henegar, Robert D. Jones, Susan Lutz, James C. Petty, David Powlison, Darby A. Strickland, Paul David Tripp, Edward T. Welch, and John Yenchko.

ADD
Anger
Angry at God?
Bad Memories
Depression
Domestic Abuse
Forgiveness
God's Love
Guidance
Homosexuality
"Just One More"
Marriage
Motives
OCD
Pornography

Pre-Engagement
Priorities
Procrastination
Prodigal Children
Self-Injury
Sexual Sin
Stress
Suffering
Suicide
Teens and Sex
Thankfulness
Why Me?
Why Worry?
Worry

See all the books and booklets in the Resources for Changing Lives series at www.prpbooks.com

MORE ON DOMESTIC ABUSE

What can counselors and concerned family and friends do when a loved one's marriage is abusive?

Darby Strickland demonstrates how to recognize and uncover oppression, then uses Scripture to show what is truly happening in abusive marriages. She equips us to be wise and informed as we confront oppressors and advocate for the oppressed.

Learn how to walk patiently with victims and guide abusers toward repentance, through Strickland's concrete suggestions for reorienting the heart of the oppressor while comforting and protecting the oppressed.

ALSO IN THE RCL SERIES

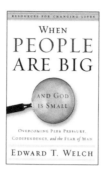

"Ed Welch is a good physician of the soul. This book is enlightening, convicting, and encouraging. I highly recommend it."

—JERRY BRIDGES

"Refreshingly biblical. . . . Brimming with helpful, readable, practical insight."

—JOHN MACARTHUR

"Readable and refreshing. . . . Goes to the heart of an issue immobilizing the church. Exposes and repudiates the trivia of therapeutic theology with wisdom and compassion."

—SUSAN HUNT